Copyright ©2007 by Downhome Publishing Inc.
43 James Lane
St. John's, NL, Canada, A1E 3H3
Tel: 1-888-588-6353
Fax: 1-709-726-2135
Web site: www.downhomelife.com
E-mail: mail@downhomelife.com

Printed in Canada

ISBN: 1-895109-34-5

Downhome Reflections

Photos from the readers
of Downhome magazine

Photo by Lynn Marsh
Orleans, ON

Berry picking with dad
(Near Botwood)

Photo by John Bolt
St. John's, NL

Blueberry bush

Photo by Doug Morris
Revelstoke, BC

Dories in waiting
(Clarenville)

Photo by Amanda Buckle
Forteau, NL

Hike around the bottom of
the Battery (Labrador)

Photo by Glenn Ivany
Burks Falls, ON

View of the old lighthouse
at Cape Spear

Photo by Donna Maloney
Torbay, NL

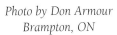

Cleaning the catch
(Sweet Bay, BB)

Photo by Gloria Young
Botwood, NL

Two-storey cellar (Maberly)

Photo by Don Armour
Brampton, ON

Corner Brook in summer

Photo by Erica Laurentius
Toronto, ON

An evening summer cruise
(Conception Bay)

Photo by Kay Locke
Fredericton, NB

Codroy Valley sunset

Photo by Collett Baker
Grand Bank, NL

Sunset over Grand Bank
Cape (Grand Bank)

Photo by Wade Foote
Foxtrap, NL

Rainbow over Big Bear
Cave Pond, Indian Bay

Photo by Tom Sykes
Appleton, Wisconsin

Lounging at the cabin
(Locker's Bay)

Photo by Steve Cooney
Eastport, NL

Dory in still waters
(Powells Cove)

Photo by Liz Pawson
Parker's Cove, NL

Weathered stage
(Parker's Cove)

Photo by Jim Hull
Pasadena, NL

Fireweed and Daisies
(Pilley's Island)

Photo by Caroline Latham
Clarenville, NL

Hollyberry raindrops
(Britannia)

Photo by Kevin Canning
Paradise, NL

Beachhead iris over
the "Dungeon"
(Cape Bonavista)

Photo by Suzanne Burden
Peterborough, ON

Boil-up on the beach
(Three Arms Bay)

Photo by Dwayne Lewis
Paradise, NL

Close-up of the bluebell
flower

Photo by Larry Chaytor
Conception Bay South, NL

A different looking
potato garden
(Cappahayden)

Photo by Dwayne Lewis
Paradise, NL

Splitting table with colour

Photo by Rick Sutton
Brampton, ON

Purpose fulfilled
(Brigus)

Photo by Desmond Pink
Halifax, NS

Line in a barrel

Photo by Christopher House
Nepean, ON

"Teach a man to fish..."
(Lobster Cove)

Photo by Mason Phillip Smith
Cape Elizabeth, ME

She has seen better days
(Mayberly)

Photo by Leon Porter
Shoal Harbour, NL

It just fits (Shoe Cove)

Photo by Dwight Hibbs
Clarenville, NL

Jamming at the cabin
(Burgoynes Cove)

Photo by Don Dormody
Grand Falls-Windsor, NL

Community bonfire in
Grand Falls-Windsor

Photo by Dean Cull
Change Islands, NL

Splitting table
(Change Islands)

Photo by Derrick Mercer
Burgeo, NL

Cooking the catch of the day
(South West Brook)

Photo by Doug Piercey
St. John's, NL

Mug up time

Photo by Heather Kidney
St. John's, NL

Sea Stacks

Photo by Heather Kidney
St. John's, NL

The Spout

Photo by Benson Jacobs
Fort McMurray, AB

The Pinnacle
(Salt Water Pond, White Bay)

Photo by John Moss
Toronto, ON

Calm before the storm
(Happy Adventure)

Photo by Kevin Kroeker
St. John's, NL

Cannons overlooking
St. John's Harbour

Table Mountains shadowing
a big pond (Cape Ray)

Beautiful summer's day
(South East Arm Placentia)

Middle Cove beach in winter

Photo by Doug Wells
Harbour Breton, NL
The Barasway
(Harbour Breton)

Photo by Geoff Smith
St. John's, NL
Middle Cove after the storm

Photo by Hans Havermann
York, ON

Laundry and lobster pots

Photo by Audrey Stringer
Mount Pearl, NL

Red Indian Lake

Photo by Don Armour
Brampton, ON

Three boats out of the water
(Cox's Cove)

Photo by Dwayne Lewis
Paradise, NL

Sunset at Swan Island

Photo by Tina Norris
St. John's, NL

The simple life
(Paddy's Pond near St. John's)

Photo by Mary Bowman
Ottawa, ON

The "Cribbies"
(Tors Cove)

Photo by Scott Young
Botwood, NL

Preparing for winter

Photo by Cassondra Hodder
Calgary, AB

Magnificent whale breach
(Petty Harbour)

Photo by Thomas Hodder
Paradise, NL

Waves breaking
on Cape Spear

Photo by Margaret Gale
South Branch, NL

Table Mountains backdrop
for the infamous Wreckhouse

Photo by Bert Hudson
Pinware, NL

Inuksuk on "Bogey's Hill"
(Pinware, Labrador)

Photo by Unknown
Moose and Fluffy

Photo by Chris Anstey
Grand Falls-Windsor, NL

Close encounter with a
moose (Twin Lakes)

Photo by Chuck Pardy
Oakville, ON

Having a yarn on the wharf
(Bonne Bay)

Photo by Walt Gill
Gander, NL

Wooden walkway
(McCallum)

Photo by Jennifer Normore
Cambridge, ON

A beautiful evening stroll
along the beach (La Scie)

Photo by Brenda LaFitte
Fox Island River, NL

Steaming towards the sunset

Photo by Caroline Latham
Clarenville, NL

Calling it a day
(Random Island)

Photo by Wanda Willcott
Labrador City, NL

Red sky at night
(South East Arm, Labrador City)

Photo by Quinton Simms
Mary's Harbour, NL

A fall's day at the cabin
(Hatters Cove)

Photo by Jennifer Morey
Port Anson, NL

A day on the boat with
flag in tow (Port Anson)

Photo by Jean Lane
Gambo, NL

The Gambo Trestle in Fall

Photo by Geoff Smith
St. John's, NL

Fence in winter
(Middle Cove)

Photo by Katharina Gale
Kentville, NS

Hampden house
(White Bay)

Photo by Tom Solomon
Westerville, OH

Rocky Harbour, below
the lighthouse

Photo by Travis Parsons
Grand Bank, NL

The Grand Bank dory races

Photo by Travis Parsons
Grand Bank, NL

Majestic waterfall
(Bowering Park, St. John's)

Photo by Mary Elizabeth Powell
St. John's, NL

Footpath along the
Rennie's River (St. John's)

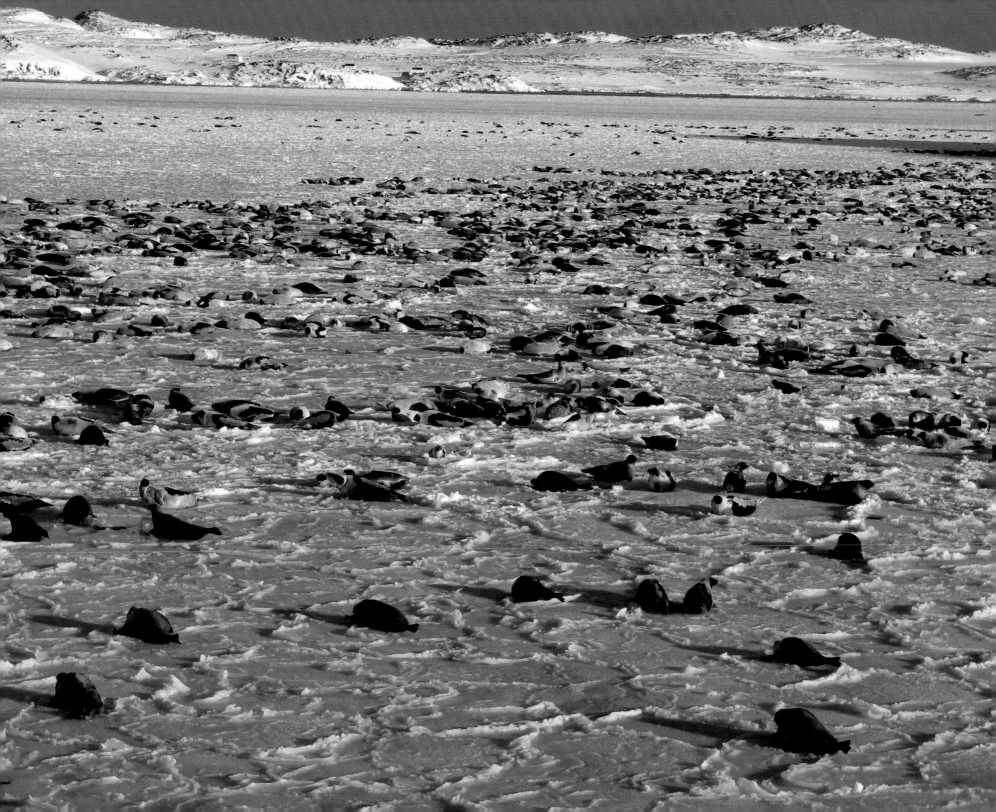

Photo by Tim Coombs
Unknown

Harps basking in the sun
(Domino Run)

Photo by Leonie Mitchell
Queensland, Australia

Signal Hill Tattoo
(St. John's)

A Newfoundland delicacy
(St. John's)

Fanny's tasty toutons
(Twillingate)

Christmas baking

Photo by Glenda Baker
Gambo, NL

A perfect summer day near
Western Bay

Photo by Lorelei Billings
Portugal Cove-St. Phillips, NL

Standing the test of time
(Kingston CB)

Photo by Brenda Decker
Fort McMurray, AB

Red Island
(Port au Port)

Photo by Eldon Roul
St. John's, NL

Sunset at St. Lawrence
(Burin Peninsula)

Photo by Roger Parsons
Little Bay, NL

Sunset at Coffee Cove

Photo by Dan & Tracey Sloan
Belleville, ON

Beautiful day on
Western Brook Pond
(Gros Morne)

Photo by Bob Hanley
Invermere, BC

Newtown Church
(Newtown, BB)

Photo by Mike Coachman
Brooksville, FL, USA

Puffin Colony

Photo by Fred Perry
St. John's, NL

Ruffed grouse by the roadside

Photo by Brent Northcott
Whitecourt, AB

Horses with Cape Anguille
lighthouse in the background

Photo by Lisa Young
Mount Moriah, NL

Winter Partridge

Photo by Darren Brocklehurst
Sarnia, ON

Cape Spear lighthouse with
Scademia in the background

Photo by Kris Reid
Innisfil, ON

Iceberg in Deep Bay

Photo by Gavin Simms
Hermitage, NL

Fog rolling in on Hermitage

Photo by Dave Bowdridge
St. John's, NL

Island coming out of the fog
(near Brigus)

Photo by Theresa Stockley
Unknown

Even the moose are
going to Alberta
(Argentia ferry terminal)

Photo by Jennifer Morey
Port Anson, NL

Hiding out
(Port Anson)

Photo by E. Eastman
Unknown

Moose eating or praying in
front of the church, you decide

Photo by Doug Piercey
St. John's, NL

A November moonlit night
(near Harbour Breton)

Photo by Christa McGrath
Torbay, NL

Nice summer's day
(Wesleyville)

Photo by Travis Parsons
Grand Bank, NL

Clinging to the "Rock"
(Quidi Vidi village)

Photo by Rhonda Pittman
Marystown, NL

Kirby's Cove stages

Photo by Liza Janes
Bridgewater, NS

Squid jigging in South Dildo
(Trinity Bay)

Photo by Glenda Baker
Gambo, NL

Lovely Greenspond
(Bonavista Bay)

Photo by Unknown

Large humpback gliding
to the water's edge

*Photo by Liza Janes,
Bridgewater, NS*

Wigwam Rock
(Dildo Island, TB)

*Photo by Tony Dean
Northern Arm, NL*

Riding and swimming
with a beluga whale
(Leading Tickles)

*Photo by Leonie Mitchell
Queensland, Australia*

Vintage wharf in Springdale

Photo by Scott Young
Botwood, NL

St. Paul's Church, Trinity

Photo by Doreen Thompson
Whaletown, BC

House of neon colours
(Round Harbour)

Photo by Troy Pearce
Grande Prairie, AB

A faithful friend to many
(The Arches Provincial
Park, GNP)

Photo by Lois Leveen
Portland, OR

Crab gear in waiting
(Mary's Harbour)

Photo by Chris Roberts
Fortune, NL

One last bit of fishing
before the day ends
(Lord's Cove)

Photo by Derrick Turner
Paradise, NL

Help, I caught a big one

Photo by Wanda Lundrigan
Glovertown, NL

By the beach reading the
Downhome magazine
(Glovertown)

Photo by Boyd Legge
Mount Pearl, NL

Squid jigging in
Heart's Delight
(Trinity Bay)

Photo by Rhonda Pittman
Marystown, NL

Squid on the line
(Marystown)

Photo by Safron Bennett
St. Paul's, NL

Suset at St. Paul's
(Northern Peninsula)

Photo by Bill Dorey
Barrie, ON

Father and son watch
the day end (Gros Morne)

Photo by Desmond Pink
Halifax, NS

Catcher in the marsh
(Peter Strides Lake)

Photo by Caroline Latham
Clarenville, NL

Pitcher plant blossom

Photo by Amy Newport
Mount Pearl, NL

Lilacs in the garden
(Mount Pearl)

Photo by Chris Dillon
Portugal Cove-St. Philips, NL

Footbridge in Lumsden

Photo by Ben Brake
South Branch, NL

Cranberry hunting on
South Branch barrens

Photo by Al Pitcher
Pasadena, NL

Snowmobile trip to
Gros Morne Park

Photo by Wayne McKenzie
Port au Port, NL

Coming through
Rocky Harbour

Photo by Ruth Grimes
Paradise, NL

Camping at Kona Beach

Photo by Frank Bastow
St. John's, NL

Waterfall at Fox Marsh on
the Avalon Peninsula

Photo by Judy Skeffington
Musgravetown, NL

Rainbow arches in
Musgravetown

Photo by Colin Buckland
St. John's, NL

Out for a quick cruise
on the bay

Photo by Brandon Ryan
Labrador City, NL

Northern lights over
Labrador City

Photo by Cathy Horlick
Sutton, ON

Colourful row housing
(St. John's)

Photo by Sean Stone -
St. John's, NL

View of St. John's from
Signal Hill

Photo by Kevin Kroeker
St. John's, NL

St. John's city skyline

Photo by Don Shorock
Great Bend, KS

George Street Festival
(St. John's)